Spotlight on the
MAYA, AZTEC, and INCA CIVILIZATIONS

Ancient
AZTEC
GOVERNMENT

Christine Honders

PowerKiDS press™

NEW YORK

Published in 2017 by The Rosen Publishing Group, Inc.
29 East 21st Street, New York, NY 10010

Editor: Katie Kawa
Book Design: Tanya Dellaccio

Photo Credits: Cover, p. 25 De Agostini Picture Library/Getty Images; p. 4 pavalena/Shutterstock.com; p. 5 George Chan/Getty Images; p. 6 https://commons.wikimedia.org/wiki/File:Flag_of_Mexico.svg; p. 7 https://commons.wikimedia.org/wiki/File:Codex_Mendoza_folio_2r.jpg; p. 8 https://commons.wikimedia.org/wiki/File:Murales_Rivera_-_Markt_in_Tlatelolco_3.jpg; p. 9 https://commons.wikimedia.org/wiki/File:Aztec_Triple_Alliance.png; p. 11 DEA/G. DAGLI ORTI/Getty Images; p. 13 Leemage/Getty Images; p. 14 https://commons.wikimedia.org/wiki/File:Acamapichtli,_the_First_Aztec_King_(Reigned_1376%E2%80%9395)_WDL6718.png; p. 15 https://commons.wikimedia.org/wiki/File:Codex_Mendoza_folio_47r.jpg; p. 16 Charles Phelps Cushing/ClassicStock/Getty Images; p. 17 https://commons.wikimedia.org/wiki/File:Cuauht%C3%A9moc.png; p. 19 https://commons.wikimedia.org/wiki/File:Cihuacoatl_statue_(Museo_Nacional_Antropologia).JPG; p. 21 (both) Dorling Kindersley/Getty Images; p. 22 fototehnik/Shutterstock.com; p. 23 Hulton Archive/Stringer/Getty Images; p. 26 https://commons.wikimedia.org/wiki/File:Codex_Mendoza_folio_69r.jpg; p. 27 https://commons.wikimedia.org/wiki/File:Miquiztli.jpg; p. 29 De Agostini/ A. Dagli Orti/Getty Images.

Library of Congress Cataloging-in-Publication Data

Names: Honders, Christine, author.
Title: Ancient Aztec government / Christine Honders.
Description: New York : PowerKids Press, 2016. | Series: Spotlight on the
  maya, aztec, and inca civilizations | Includes index.
Identifiers: LCCN 2016006675 | ISBN 9781499419146 (pbk.) | ISBN 9781499419214 (library bound) | ISBN 9781499419191 (6 pack)
Subjects: LCSH: Aztecs--Politics and government--Juvenile literature.
Classification: LCC F1219.76.P75 H66 2016 | DDC 320.972--dc23
LC record available at http://lccn.loc.gov/2016006675

CPSIA Compliance Information: Batch #BS16PK For further information contact Rosen Publishing, New York, New York at 1-800-237-9932.

CONTENTS

A POWERFUL EMPIRE

The Aztec Empire was the last native Mesoamerican empire to flourish before Europeans arrived in the Americas. Mesoamerica stretched over part of the area that's now known as Central America and the southern part of North America. During the 14th, 15th, and 16th centuries, the Aztec people came to rule much of the land in present-day central and southern Mexico.

The Aztecs were masters of farming, and this allowed them to develop a successful civilization that grew into a powerful empire. Their capital city had the largest population in all of Mesoamerica, and thousands of people came to sell and trade goods in Aztec marketplaces.

UNITED STATES

PACIFIC OCEAN

MEXICO

■ MESOAMERICA

Much of what we know about the Aztec people—including their government—has come from the study of Aztec ruins found in Mexico, such as those shown here.

Because of their agricultural and economic success, the Aztecs were able to build a powerful government that ruled as many as 500 **city-states** and up to 6 million people. The Aztec people's system of government was well organized and helped hold the growing empire together.

WHERE DID THEY COME FROM?

No one is exactly sure where the Aztec people came from. It's believed they were a group of **nomadic** hunter-gatherers from northern Mexico. Aztec legends state that their original homeland was called Aztlán. These nomads arrived in the Valley of Mexico around 1250.

According to legend, the god Huitzilopochtli told the nomads to look for a place where an eagle was perched on a cactus, killing a snake. After many years, the people saw this sign from their god near Lake Texcoco. They made this spot their permanent home. Before this time, these nomads had never settled in one place long enough to develop any kind of advanced government. That was about to change. They began to set up a government and build what would become the most powerful Mesoamerican empire of its time.

MEXICAN FLAG

The modern Mexican government honors the country's Aztec roots with its flag. The Mexican flag shows the famous eagle, snake, and cactus from the ancient Aztec legends.

ESTABLISHING AN EMPIRE

In 1325, the Aztecs established their capital city, which was named Tenochtitlán, on an island in Lake Texcoco. This doesn't seem like an ideal place to live, but the Aztecs were smart. They built canoes to make it easier to travel and fish. They drained much of the swamp, built artificial islands with reeds and mud, and developed **irrigation** systems to create more farmland and grow more crops. The Aztec people's farming methods made Tenochtitlán a wealthy city with a growing population.

Tenochtitlán was the center of the Aztec government. The leader of the Aztec Empire lived there.

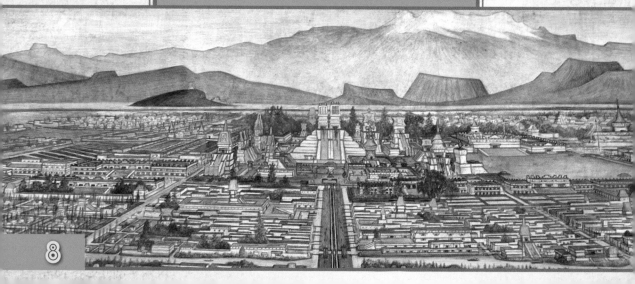

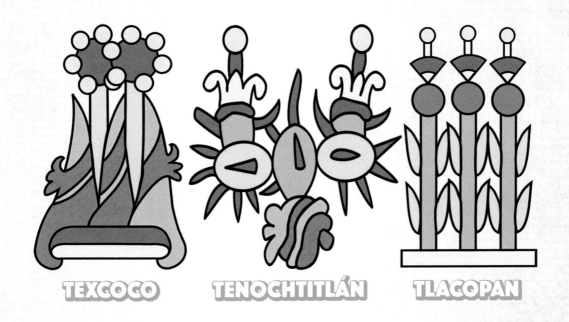

TEXCOCO   TENOCHTITLÁN   TLACOPAN

Pictures similar to these may have represented the members of the Triple Alliance in Aztec writings.

As the population of Tenochtitlán grew, Aztec leaders set their sights on the lands beyond this island city. In 1428, under the leadership of Itzcóatl, the Aztec people of Tenochtitlán formed an alliance with two nearby states: Texcoco and Tlacopan. This is often called the Triple Alliance. They began conquering nearby groups and using their natural resources to grow more powerful. An empire was born!

THE FOUNDATION OF AZTEC GOVERNMENT

The family unit was the base of Aztec society. The first level of Aztec government was called the calpulli. Each of these was most often made up of groups of families that shared a piece of land. The calpulli system was part of Aztec **culture** long before the empire reached its height, and it eventually extended to the farthest reaches of the empire's lands.

There's a lot of confusion about the calpulli system because there are few written records concerning it. Something that historians agree on is that each of the many calpulli had a council of elders and a main leader.

The calpulli set up schools, which were called telpuchcalli. The calpulli also had their own temples and government buildings. Warriors from each calpulli fought together during times of war. The leaders kept track of calpulli members, gave lands to families, and collected taxes.

The calpulli were the building blocks of Aztec society and government. A large Aztec city, such as Tenochtitlán (shown here), was made up of many calpulli.

Some scholars describe the calpulli as tribal, landholding groups based on family membership. Others believe the calpulli were made up of groups of Aztec commoners under the control of the same group of **nobles**. The city-states of the Aztec Empire were made up of several calpulli, similar to neighborhoods in today's large cities. Each of the calpulli had its own god who was supposed to watch over its people.

In the city-states, the leaders of the calpulli made up the city council. The city council would then choose the members of an executive council. One member of the executive council was the *tlatoani*, or the leader of the city-state. This leader always came from the noble class of Aztec society. As the empire grew and city-states became more powerful, the government became less of a democracy and more of a monarchy. People had less of a say in choosing their leaders.

There were many different levels of Aztec government. Councils existed for the calpulli, the city-states, and the whole empire. Shown here is an illustration of a meeting of the council that governed the entire Aztec Empire.

A CITY-STATE SYSTEM

Each Aztec city-state was known as an *altepetl*. City-states were made up of a central city that controlled several surrounding towns. The *tlatoani* led the military, was the head of the temple and market, and had final judgment in legal matters throughout his city-state. The *tlatoani* also appointed others to government positions. The tax collectors, or *calpixque*, collected goods and services from the members of the calpulli.

Shown here is a drawing of Acamapichtli, who's believed to have been the first *tlatoani* of Tenochtitlán.

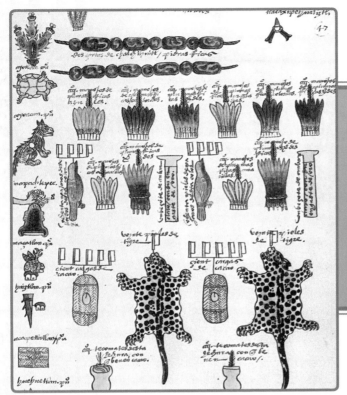

When different city-states became part of the Aztec Empire—most often through conquest—they began paying tribute to the emperor. This page from an Aztec codex, or book of ancient writings, shows different items offered as tribute.

Each city-state was ruled from afar by the emperor, who lived in Tenochtitlán. The emperor was the *tlatoani* of the capital city. The emperor generally wouldn't interfere with the city-states as long as tribute was paid. Tribute is payment made to a ruler as a sign of loyalty, respect, and peace. Tributes could be food, other goods, and even slaves. Because the emperor generally left the local governments alone, the Aztec Empire is sometimes called a **hegemonic** empire instead of a territorial empire.

THE *HUEY TLATOANI*

The ruler of Tenochtitlán was called the *huey tlatoani*. The *huey tlatoani* was the ultimate ruler of the Aztec Empire, so he's also called the emperor. The Aztecs believed he had a direct connection to the gods, which was important because religion was a central part of Aztec life.

Shown here is Montezuma II, who was the *huey tlatoani* at the time of the Spanish conquest of Aztec lands.

Shown here is Cuauhtémoc, who was the last emperor of the Aztecs.

The Aztecs expanded their territory through war, and the emperor decided where and when to go to battle. Only accomplished warriors could hold this position. The emperor also had to be a member of the noble class, which received the best education in the empire.

The emperor had absolute power, but it's believed at least one emperor was killed after falling out of favor with the Aztec people. Historians believe Aztec emperors ruled by fear. This caused hatred among many neighboring groups and people the Aztecs conquered. These people then turned on the empire when the Spanish arrived years later.

POWERFUL POSITIONS

After the emperor, the next highest official in the Aztec government was the *cihuacoatl*. While the emperor oversaw the entire empire, the *cihuacoatl* was responsible for the day-to-day operations of government in Tenochtitlán. He appointed judges to positions in the Aztec court system and handled Tenochtitlán's finances. The *cihuacoatl* was always a noble. He was always a family member of the emperor, too. Women couldn't serve as the *cihuacoatl* or as any other government leader.

The *cihuacoatl* gave advice to the emperor. The emperor also had a council of four advisors, which some historians call the Council of Four. The men who served on this council—like the members of the executive councils in all Aztec city-states—were members of the noble class. This council also selected a new ruler after an emperor died. They most often chose the new emperor from the brothers or other family members of the previous ruler.

The position of *cihuacoatl* was named after the Aztec goddess Cihuacóatl, even though the office was always held by a man. Shown here is a statue of Cihuacóatl.

AZTEC NOBLES

The noble class held the most power in Aztec government and society. The nobles in Tenochtitlán and other city-states acted as judges, priests, and military leaders. Sometimes they were appointed as rulers of a conquered city.

Aztec nobles were given many privileges, including education at their own special schools. While all Aztec children went to school, the children of nobles went to a school that taught them to be leaders. They learned what they needed to know to hold a government position. Nobles also lived in larger homes than Aztec commoners. They were allowed to wear colorful clothing with many decorations, while commoners had to wear plain clothing. However, being a noble didn't guarantee a person a government position. Some nobles were landowners but not government officials.

Nobles didn't have to pay taxes. Instead, they received tributes from commoners who lived on their lands.

AZTEC NOBLES

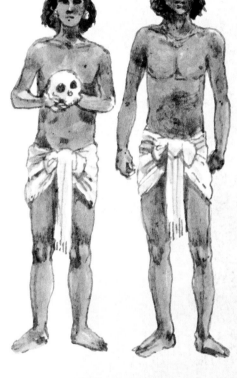

AZTEC SLAVES

Aztec nobles were allowed to wear clothing with feathers, beads, and bright colors. Commoners and slaves mostly wore simple, white clothes. This helped make the difference between nobles and members of the lower classes clear to everyone in the empire.

RELIGION AND GOVERNMENT

While some Aztec commoners could be priests, the highest Aztec priests were part of the noble class. They had a great deal of power in the government. In modern times, the idea of "separation of church and state" is the law of the land. In Aztec society, however, that idea didn't exist. The emperor was the head of the Aztec religion. The high priest of the sun god and the high priest of the rain god were also very important.

AZTEC SUN STONE

Aztec priests kept the calendar, and they carried out human sacrifices to please their gods. Many of the people sacrificed came from conquered lands, and this practice helped the emperor rule by fear.

Aztec priests were in charge of religious ceremonies, naming new priests, and taking care of the temple lands. They were also responsible for running Aztec schools.

Religion was so important in Aztec culture that it controlled the government. The priests communicated the gods' wishes to the government leaders. The leaders then ruled the empire based on what they believed would keep the gods happy.

AZTEC LAW

Aztec law focused on keeping order in the social system and maintaining respect for the government. Laws were based on orders from the emperor and customs passed down through generations. Criminal and civil laws were sometimes written down in the picture language used by the Aztecs, and sometimes they were passed down **orally**.

Aztec laws covered marriage, divorce, **inheritances**, and even the class system. A married man could have many wives, but only the children of his first, or primary, wife could inherit his estate. In certain situations, divorce was allowed by Aztec law, and the wife was sometimes allowed to get half the couple's property and could remarry. Crimes were dealt with using a court system with different levels, much like the system we have in the United States today. However, juries didn't exist in the Aztec Empire. Instead, judges had the final say in every case.

The Aztec legal system didn't make use of lawyers. The person accused of a crime spoke for themselves in front of the judges. They could also bring a family member or friend to plead their case. Shown here is a page from an Aztec codex depicting an Aztec emperor and his council (top), as well as Aztec judges (bottom).

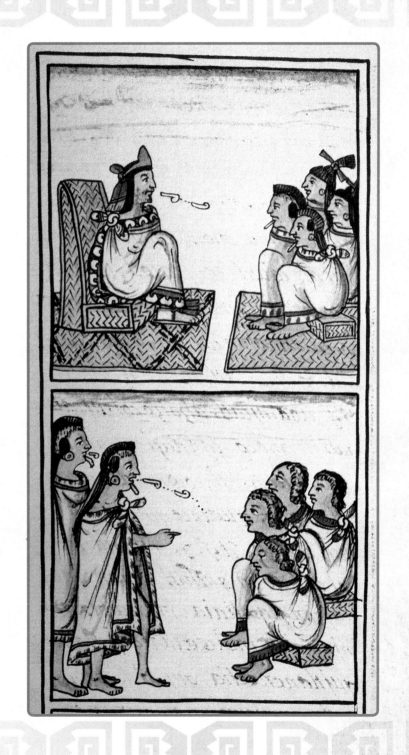

CRIME AND PUNISHMENT

There were several main levels in the Aztec court system. Local courts had elected judges that dealt with minor offenses. If a crime was more serious or if the ruling of the court was questioned, the case would go to the *teccalli* court in that city-state. *Teccalli* judges were appointed by Aztec leaders. Another level of the Aztec court system was a kind of

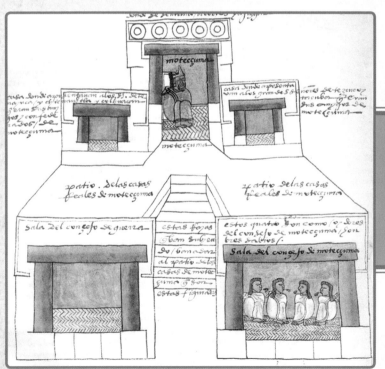

This page from an Aztec codex shows the emperor at the top and a group of judges in the bottom right corner.

supreme court, which was **presided** over by the *cihuacoatl*. If the *cihuacoatl* felt it was necessary, he sent cases to the emperor. The emperor had the right to participate in any ruling he felt was important to the empire.

The death penalty was common and not just used to punish murderers. It was also used in cases of stealing, destroying crops, witchcraft, and selling stolen goods, among many other crimes. Common methods of **execution** were stoning, hanging, or drowning. Lesser crimes were punishable by shaving the criminal's head, a sentence of slavery, or many punishments in between.

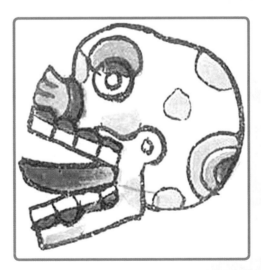

Shown here is an Aztec drawing meant to represent death, which was the punishment for many crimes committed in the Aztec Empire.

THE END OF AN EMPIRE

Spanish **conquistador** Hernán Cortés landed on what's now the Mexican coast in April 1519, during the reign of the Aztec emperor Montezuma II. A representative of Montezuma greeted Cortés with gifts. However, Cortés wasn't looking to make a friendly alliance with the Aztec people. He wanted to take over their lands in the name of the Spanish government.

Cortés and his forces marched toward Tenochtitlán, conquering city-states as they went. The Tlaxcalans, who were another native Mesoamerican group, eventually allied with Cortés because they hated the Aztecs. When Cortés got to Tenochtitlán, he was given more gifts and invited into the emperor's palace. The Spanish held Montezuma captive inside the palace. The emperor died while being held prisoner.

The Aztecs then drove Cortés and his army out of Tenochtitlán. However, Cortés returned and took over the city for good in 1521. The Aztec Empire had fallen.

This painting shows the brutal battle fought between the Aztecs and the Spanish for control of Tenochtitlán.

29

THE LAST OF ITS KIND

When Cortés and his forces took over Tenochtitlán, the city was at its height, with more than 140,000 people living there. The Aztec Empire had a bustling economy and a ruling government that was more **complex** and organized than any other in the history of Mesoamerica. If the Spanish hadn't arrived when they did, the Aztec Empire might have continued to grow. However, the Spanish brought warfare and disease to the Aztec world, killing large numbers of Aztec people.

The Aztec Empire was the last great Mesoamerican empire to exist before the Spanish came to that part of the world. Although the Aztec government was taken over by the Spanish, not everything about this great civilization was lost. Artifacts, ruins, and written records from the past have helped us piece together what it was like to live under the rule of the Aztec government.

GLOSSARY

city-state (SIH-tee–STAYT): A self-governing state made up of a city and surrounding lands.

complex (kahm-PLEHKS): Having many parts.

conquistador (kahn-KEES-tuh-dor): A Spanish leader who conquered, or took over, people and land in the Americas during the 16th century.

culture (KUHL-chuhr): The beliefs and ways of life of a certain group of people.

execution (ek-suh-KYOO-shuhn): A putting to death as legal punishment.

hegemonic (heh-juh-MAA-nihk): Relating to influence or control one nation or group has over others without the use of direct military control.

inheritance (in-HEHR-uh-tuhns): Something a person gets after a person in their family dies.

irrigation (eer-uh-GAY-shun): The supplying of water to land by man-made means.

noble (NOH-buhl): A person who belongs to a high social class.

nomadic (noh-MAA-dihk): Having no fixed home and wandering from place to place.

orally (OR-uh-lee): Spoken in words.

preside (prih-ZYD): To be in a position of authority at a meeting, gathering, or ceremony.

INDEX

PRIMARY SOURCE LIST

Page 7: Folio 2 of the Codex Mendoza. Creator unknown. ca. 1542. Now kept at the Bodleian Library, Oxford University, Oxford, UK.

Page 15: Folio 47 of the Codex Mendoza. Creator unknown. ca. 1542. Now kept at the Bodleian Library, Oxford University, Oxford, UK.

Page 25: Page from the Florentine Codex. Compiled by Fray Bernardino de Sahagún. ca. 1529–1588. Now kept at the Laurentian Library, Florence, Italy.

Page 26: Folio 69 of the Codex Mendoza. Creator unknown. ca. 1542. Now kept at the Bodleian Library, Oxford University, Oxford, UK.

WEBSITES

Due to the changing nature of Internet links, PowerKids Press has developed an online list of websites related to the subject of this book. This site is updated regularly. Please use this link to access the list: www.powerkidslinks.com/soac/azgov